T0194920

GREATEST
TIPS ABOUT
POOL
YOU NEED
TO KNOW

GEORGE MOYLE

authorHOUSE®

AuthorHouse™
1663 Liberty Drive
Bloomington, IN 47403
www.authorhouse.com
Phone: 1 (800) 839-8640

Published by AuthorHouse 07/29/2019

ISBN: 978-1-7283-2130-1 (sc)
ISBN: 978-1-7283-2129-5 (e)

CONTENTS

INTRODUCTION

Boy, what a struggle it can be when you don't have someone to help you learn the game of pool. When I was a young man trying to learn the game, no one would help me with anything, and those who thought they knew what they were talking about made no sense at all. I found out right away that all that the good players wanted was my money, and the other players wanted people to think they knew what they were doing. They were good—yeah, they made a lot of balls—but when it came to a tournament, those guys couldn't make a ball to save their lives. They didn't know how to cope with the pressure. They folded and never made a ball. You want to know how to cope with the pressure and not think about it. You need this book. If you want to be good, it's good to have someone helping you to give you some hints and instructions on how to be good. But it boils down to good old-fashioned practice, practice, practice. So guess what?

I spent a lot of my days at the pool table just relaxing and hitting balls, day after day for hours on end. I never forced myself to learn about English. I just wanted to relax and hit balls. The day came, though, when I asked myself, *What would the cue ball do if I just did this or that?* I started trying to use some English on just about every shot, whether the English was right or wrong, just to find out what the English would do with a certain shot. Of course, I had it all wrong at that point. I thought that if I did a certain thing, the cue ball would do a certain other thing. It didn't. Sometimes I didn't understand what I had done at all or why the cue ball had done what it did. Boy, at first, English was Greek to me! One of the things I found out is that to understand English, you have to keep after it every day and remember what you have done. Talk about spending hours on the pool table! But that's what it takes. When you have someone helping you, it takes some of the agony away. You can understand what you're trying to accomplish by working with an instructor. When you don't have someone helping you, it's a long and hard process. If you think that pool isn't work, I'm here to tell you that is far from the truth. It takes a lot of hard work to become a good pool player. It involves discipline, being serious about the game, some long hours, and days of practice. It takes work. I was working a forty-hour job, was married, and was raising one, then two, and then three kids, and I still found time to play pool and practice. Eventually, I became one of the best players around. Then came the day when my wife and I had our fourth child—no more time for pool! I knew that I had to spend some time with my family, so I gave up pool for a good while, not playing in any tournaments or doing any gambling. But I missed the game so much that I just had to come back.

I hope my book will help you become a person to be reckoned with.

Practice hard and long.

CHAPTER 1

THE QUARTER BALL SYSTEM

On these next few pages, I will introduce you to what I call the quarter ball system. This system should help you with the angles you'll face when shooting the object ball for any pocket. In the quarter ball system, there are four different angles that you'll be exploring. You'll have a full-ball hit, a quarter-ball hit, a half-ball hit, and then a three-quarter-ball hit.

The Full-Ball or Center-Ball Hit

First, mentally cut the cue ball, along with the object ball, into quarters, starting at the center of both balls and working your way out to the edge.

Place two balls on the table—the cue ball and an object ball. Make sure they're straight in line with each other and in the middle of the table from side pocket to side pocket, about twenty-four inches apart. You're going to pocket the object ball into the side pocket using a full-ball hit. Mentally draw a line straight down through the center of the cue ball, and do the same with the object ball. This line through the object ball will always point to the pocket where you're playing the ball. Now, these lines that you drew through the cue ball and the object ball have to line up, straight up and down with each other, for a full-ball hit to pocket the object ball straight into the side pocket.

The question is, even though you pocketed the object ball, did you see the line that you'd drawn through the center of the cue ball? And the line in the center of the object ball is what you need to see and hit every time you shoot a center-ball shot. You need to see that center line. Did the object ball go straight into the pocket?

The Center-Ball Hit

If so, then line up for a longer shot, and practice this center-ball hit or straight-in shot. Make sure you draw a line through both balls each time that you shoot this shot. Also make sure that you see the line on both balls before shooting. This is the beginning of the quarter ball system. You always need a visual or a line of sight pointing you to the pocket where you're shooting the object ball. If you have no line of sight to the pocket, you're shooting in the dark. This system gives that line of sight that you need.

The Quarter-Ball Hit from Center

Once again, line up the object and cue balls in the same positions on the table, with both balls pointed to the side pocket. Now rotate the cue ball to the side one half of a turn. Cut the object ball with a straight line down the center, pointed straight into the side pocket. On every shot, the line that you draw down through the object ball should be pointed straight to the pocket where you're going to take the object ball. That line is what you need to hit in order to pocket the object ball. Now, since you rotated the cue ball one half of a turn, you have a quarter-ball shot, not a full-ball hit. This shot is one quarter of a ball from the center of the object ball and a quarter of a ball from the center of the cue ball. How do you determine that this is a quarter ball?

This next line you want to draw is a center line. This center line will be a full-ball hit on both balls. This line through both balls should point you to the rail, not to the pocket; this is your full-ball hit. The second line will be through the object ball to the pocket. As you can see, there are two separate lines. Now, how far from the first line you drew through the object ball (the full-ball hit) to the second line (to the pocket) do you need to hit the object ball to pocket it? You should only be off your center line (your full-ball hit) by a quarter of a ball. That's a quarter ball on the object and a quarter ball on the cue ball. These two have to match up and come together to pocket the object ball.

See the diagram below.

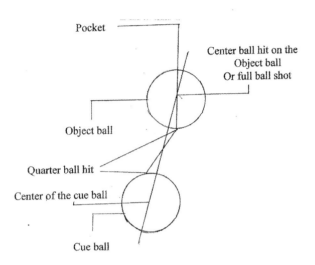

Pocket

Center ball hit on the
Object ball
Or full ball shot

Object ball

Quarter ball hit

Center of the cue ball

Cue ball

The quarter-ball system will show you just about every angle on the table, from a hard-cut shot to the simplest straight-in shots.

Place an object ball near the second diamond up from the bottom rail, one full ball away from the side rail toward the center of the table. Now place the cue ball on the first diamond from the bottom rail so that the object ball and cue ball are both along the same side rail, one diamond apart. The cue ball is the same distance from the rail as the object ball; they are straight in line with each other.

You want to pocket the object ball into the corner pocket at the other end of the table. Where's your aiming point on the object ball? Do you have an aiming point? Or are you just going to guess? The quarter-ball system takes the guesswork and the I-don't-know out of the game.

Cut the object ball into quarters. Starting at the center of the object ball and going out to its edge, there should be three different quarter cuts on the object ball. The first cut should be one quarter of a ball from the center of the object ball. This is a quarter shot. Now, cut the object ball in half again from its center. This will be a half-ball shot. Now, make one more cut, this time one quarter from the edge or outer portion of the object ball. This is your three-quarter-ball shot—three quarters of a ball from the center of your object ball.

See the diagram below.

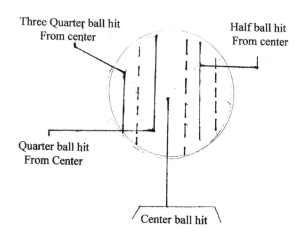

The diagram below contains five balls in reference to five shots in difference pockets. Each of these shots is a quarter-ball hit from the center of the object ball and the center of the cue ball. Notice the slight angle of the object ball to the pocket. These shots look like they're almost straight in. Here is a visual to help you see what you should look at on the object ball and the cue ball. A quarter of the cue ball has to match up with one quarter of the object ball.

See the diagram below, A and B.

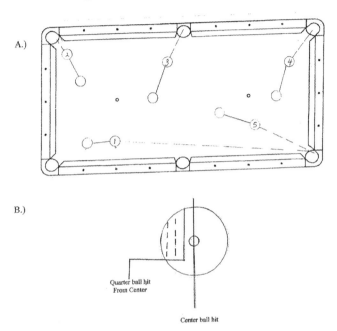

The Half-Ball Shot

The diagram below consists of four balls, each of which will be a half-ball shot. The half-ball shot is just as its name indicates—halfway from the center of the object ball to its edge. It's the same on the cue ball—halfway from the center to the edge. The two lines, one on the object ball and the other on the cue ball, must match up together line for line in order to pocket the object ball.

See the diagram below, A and B.

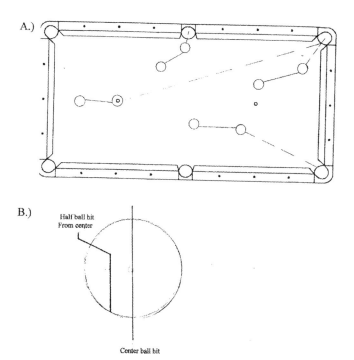

The diagram below has four balls on the table. These four balls are all three-quarter-ball shots from the center of the cue ball. In making this shot, you will hit the object ball all the way to its edge. You will do the same with the cue ball; hit it all the way out to its edge to make this shot. This is one of the hardest shots you will encounter on the table. One reason for its difficulty is that you can't get a visual on the pocket, so the only reference point you have is on the cue ball and the object ball.

See the diagram below, A and B.

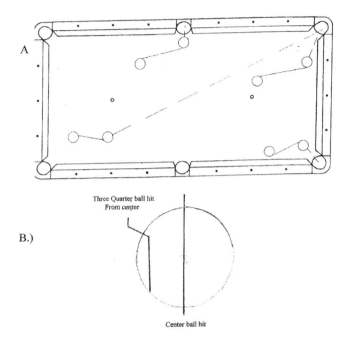

Bank Shots

Bank shots are not as hard as they look if they are off the rail. Place an object ball off the bottom rail on the left, one diamond in toward the table. Then, from the right-side rail, the same object ball needs to be in between the first diamond and the right rail. Place the cue ball down at the other end of the table just past the side pocket off the right rail, the same distance that you placed the object ball. When you've placed the two balls on the table, they should be straight in line with each other. You want to pocket the object ball into the corner pocket at the other end of the table where you placed the cue ball.

Now, for this shot, all you need to do is hit the object ball off center by one-eighth of a ball, on the opposite side to where you are going to pocket the ball. The object ball's position off the rail will allow the cue ball enough angle to pass by without being hit a second time. The second object ball is on the left side of the table next to the rail. It is up from the bottom rail one full diamond and in from the left side rail one full diamond. The cue ball is at the other end of the table two diamonds in from the bottom rail and the same distance in line with the object ball, one full diamond from the left side rail. To pocket the object ball into the corner pocket at the other end of the table where you have placed the cue ball, shoot this shot one-quarter of a ball from the center of the object ball.

Your next bank shot will be from the diamond in the center of the table, off the bottom rail. Spot the object ball at the center diamond at the bottom rail, then move the object ball up from the bottom rail one diamond in toward the table. Place the cue ball again at the other end of the table straight in line with the object ball, two diamonds up from the bottom rail. This shot will be a half-ball shot to either pocket at the other end of the table where the cue ball was placed.

See the diagrams below.

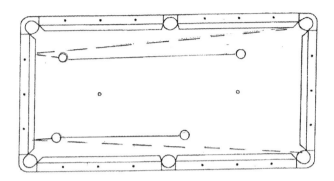

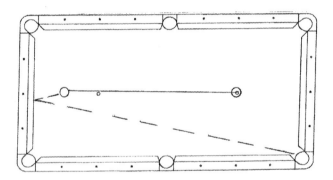

CHAPTER 2

PRACTICE SHOTS AND ROUTINES

You're going to get into some practice shots on the next few pages. You're also going to have to have some idea of the speed I want you to shoot or stroke a particular shot when doing these routines, so I included a scale that should help you. If you already have a scale to judge your speed and if you can adapt it to the practice routines, please do so; if not, please use the scale that I have provided. It should give you some idea of what I'm talking about when I say, "You need to shoot or stroke this shot at a two on a scale from one to ten." Throughout the next few pages of practice routines, in most cases I will say that—"on a scale from one to ten"—on almost every page.

Use Center English

Start at the end rail with the cue ball. Now shoot the cue ball the length of the table until it just hits the rail at the other end. That would be a one on a scale from one to ten. On your next stroke, shoot the cue ball hard enough to hit the far rail and return to the rail from where you started. That would be a two.

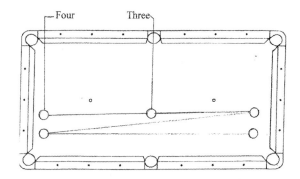

High English

Now, I want you to practice a routine that will help you with your high English. See the diagram below. Pocket the object ball and run the cue ball forward, stopping in the gray area.

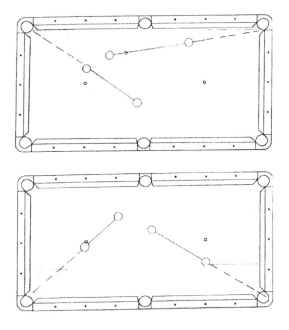

Practice Routine: High English

This routine will be a three-rail shot using high left English.

The first object ball will be located at the center of the table three inches away from the left side pocket. The cue ball will be at the center of the table, on the right side of the pocket, in between the pocket and the first diamond. The second object ball will be in the middle of the bottom rail, in toward the table one half of a diamond.

Shoot the first object ball into the side pocket with a moderate stroke, nice and smooth with high English, one tip above the center of the cue ball and with one tip of English to the left of the center of the cue ball.

The cue ball will travel three rails—to the left side rail, to the bottom rail, to the opposite side rail, and then to the other end of the table for the second object ball. Shoot this shot at a two on the scale from one to ten.

See the diagram below.

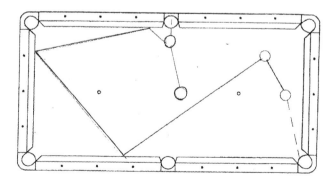

Practice Routine: High English

In this practice routine, you will be using high English and then middle English to stop the cue ball.

The first object ball will be located at the bottom rail not quite one half of a diamond off the rail. The cue ball will be placed up from the bottom rail one and a half diamonds. From the right rail, the cue ball will be off of the rail one diamond.

Shoot the first object ball with high English and pocket it into the corner pocket, using one tip of high English directly above the center of the cue ball. Use a moderate stroke and make sure that it is nice and smooth, and your follow-through should be about an inch through the cue ball. You will be running the cue ball two rails to get shape on the second object ball. For the second object ball, use middle English to stop the cue ball.

See the diagram below.

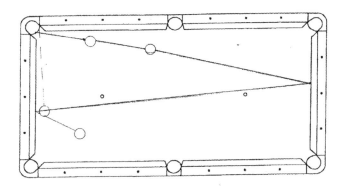

Practice Routine: High English

For this practice routine, you will use high left English on the first object ball. On the second object ball you should use low English to control the cue ball.

The first object ball will be located at the bottom rail in the center of the rail, one half of a diamond off of the rail in toward the table. The cue ball will be directly in line with the object ball one half of a diamond off of the bottom rail. The second object ball will be at the other end of the table at the center diamond, one half of a diamond up from the bottom rail.

Shoot the object ball with high left English, one full tip of high English above the center of the cue ball with left English, over to the left of the center of the cue ball one full tip. Pocket the object ball into the corner pocket. The high English will carry the cue ball to the right rail. The left English will cause the cue ball to spin off of the rail and travel down the table to the next object ball. For the second object ball, you need to use low English, about a full tip below the center of the cue ball, to control the cue ball.

See the diagram below.

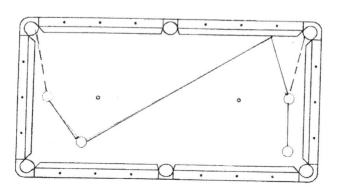

Practice Routine: High English

In this routine, you will shoot five object balls. For the first object ball, you will shoot high English. On the second, third, fourth, and fifth object balls, you will be using low English.

The first object ball will be located at the middle diamond at the bottom rail, off the rail one half of one diamond in toward the table. The cue ball will be in line with the first object ball one half of a diamond off of the bottom rail at the first diamond nearest the corner pocket.

The second object ball is at the other end of the table just off the left side rail one half of an inch and up from the bottom rail less than two diamonds.

The third object ball will be placed up from the bottom rail less than three diamonds and in from the right rail one and one half diamonds.

The fourth object ball is located at the right bottom rail two inches off the rail. From the right rail, place the ball just less than two diamonds.

The fifth and last of the object balls will be placed off of the left side rail one inch and from the bottom rail up two and one half diamonds.

Pocket the first object ball using straight high English, one tip directly above the center of the cue ball. Shoot the object ball into the corner pocket using a moderate stroke, about a two on the scale from one to ten. Run the cue ball to the right side rail, rebounding and down toward the center of the table toward the second object ball on the left side rail. The cue ball needs an angle on the second object ball so you have room to move the cue ball over for your third shot, so don't get too tight or right against that left side rail. You need to be off that left rail about six to eight inches.

Pocket the second object ball into the corner pocket and use one tip of low English directly below the center of the cue ball, coming off of the left side rail and over for the third object ball. Use a moderate stroke for this shot, no harder than a two on the scale from to ten, making sure that your stroke is nice and smooth.

Pocket the third object ball into the right side pocket using low English, one full tip directly below the center of the cue ball, to pull the cue ball over to the right side rail, down toward the fourth object ball. This shot should be a two on the scale from one to ten. You don't want the cue ball to be too close to the fourth object ball because this time you need more of an angle to get to the fifth object ball. The cue ball has to travel to the other end of the table, so leave more of an angle than you did on the other object balls so you can get up the table. Try not to run the cue ball past the first diamond nearest the corner pocket. That should give you the room you need.

For the fourth object ball you're going to use high English, one tip directly above the center of the cue ball. Shoot this shot at about a one on the scale from one to ten. The cue ball will run to the bottom rail, come off the rail, and run up the table toward the fifth object ball.

On the fifth object ball, you are going to use low English, one tip directly below the center of the cue ball. Shoot this ball at a two on the scale from one to ten, making sure that you control the cue ball. The low English will ensure that the cue ball stays somewhere in the area after pocketing the object ball.

See the diagram below.

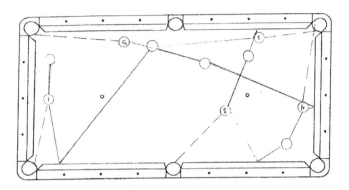

Practice Routine: High English

On this practice routine, you will be shooting high English on the first object ball. On the second object ball, use low English to stop the cue ball in the same area as the object ball.

Place the first object ball up from the bottom rail one diamond and in from the right side rail four inches, or a half of a ball.

Your second object ball will be placed down the table just past the left side pocket one diamond, or up from the bottom rail three diamonds and in from the left side rail one diamond.

The cue ball will be placed down at the other end of the table off of the right side rail one diamond and up from the bottom rail three diamonds.

You will pocket the first object ball into the corner pocket and use one half of a tip above the center of the cue ball. Run the cue ball to the bottom rail and back down to the other side of the table for the second object ball. You need a moderate stroke, about a two on the scale from one to ten.

Pocket the second object ball into the corner pocket and use low English, one and a half of a tip below the center of the cue ball to stop the cue ball.

See the diagram below.

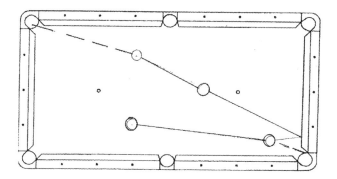

Practice routine: High English

This routine requires you to use high English on the first object ball. Then, for the second object ball, you will use low English to stop the cue ball.

The first object ball will be placed in the center of the table two inches away from the center of the side pocket. The second object ball will be at the other end of the table one half of a diamond off the bottom rail, in from the left rail one and one half of a diamond.

The cue ball will be placed just over halfway down the table, in between the side pocket and the first diamond past the pocket on the right side of the table, in from the right rail one diamond.

Pocket the first object ball and use one full tip of high English, forcing the cue ball forward to the rail just on the left side of the pocket. The cue ball will rebound and go down the table to the second object ball. For the last shot you need to use low English, one tip below the center of the cue ball to stop the ball.

See the diagram below.

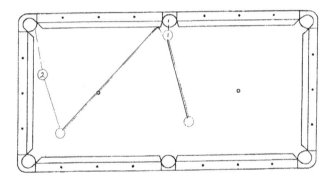

In this routine, you will use high English. Place the object ball approximately two diamonds in from the side rail. Freeze the object ball to the bottom rail. Place the cue ball on the other side of the table about one-half of a diamond off the side rail and the same distance from the bottom rail. Use high English with a moderate stroke. The cue ball should run forward and to the side rail.

See example below.

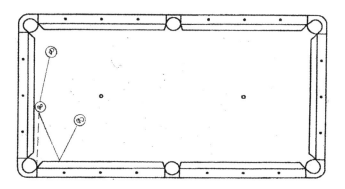

Practice Shots and Routines

This routine requires you to use high right English. Place the object ball you're going to pocket away from the side pocket roughly ten inches. The cue ball should be placed in the center of the table straight in line with the object ball. Use high right English, shooting straight at the object ball with a heavy stroke and good follow-through. The cue ball will be forced to the left of the object ball, but you will still pocket the object ball. The cue ball will spin forward with right English, strike the rail on the left side of the side pocket, and then spin back across the table to the right side of the opposite pocket.

See example below.

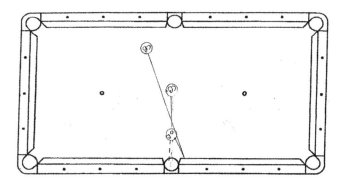

Center English

The center of the cue ball is foremost a stop shot as long as you shoot it with some speed. What the cue ball has to do in order to stop is slide across the table neither rolling forward nor spinning backward. The distance that the cue ball has to slide or travel will determine how hard you need to hit it. The greater the distance, the harder you need to hit the cue ball. Say, for instance, you're only three feet away from the object ball with the cue ball, and you want to stop the cue ball. Practice hitting the cue ball at dead center with a moderate stroke just to see if the cue ball is going to roll forward. If it does, shoot the cue ball just a little harder until you can stop it with some control. If the cue ball comes back toward you, you didn't hit it in the center. You shot it below the center and drew it back with backspin. Now, if the cue ball did roll forward—say, about six or eight inches or less—you used high English. Check your point of aim on the cue ball. That is where the cue stick is coming into contact with the ball. When the cue ball is farther away from the object ball—say, three and a half to four feet—you don't want to try to stop it by hitting it in the center. You will have to shoot it so hard that the object ball and the cue ball both go flying off the table. Your stop shot using center English should be no further than three feet. There are ways to stop the cue ball when the distance is even the full length of the table (see the section on low English). Hitting the object ball with the cue ball using center English at a slight angle will cause the cue ball to run side to side, not forward. Middle English will stop the cue ball or run it side to side, all at a short distance.

In this routine you will use center English. Place the object ball on the table at the bottom rail. Place the cue ball off the side rail approximately one half of a diamond and up from the bottom rail just shy of one diamond. Using center English, shoot this shot with a moderate stroke and a good follow-through. The cue ball should travel straight up the center of the table and back.

See the example below.

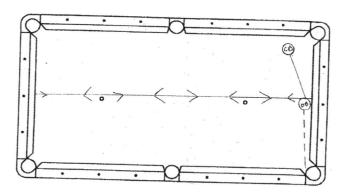

See the diagrams below.

A). Center English with an angle   B). Center English stop shot

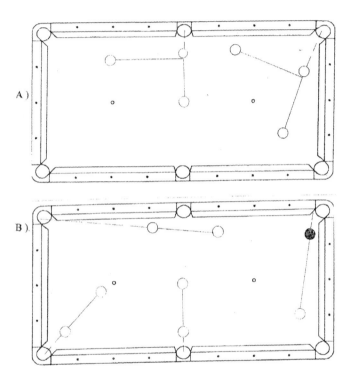

Practice routines: Draw Shots

This one-rail routine is one of the shots that you will encounter in just about every game of pool.

The first object ball will be placed off of the right side rail one half of a diamond and up from the bottom rail two full diamonds. It will be pocketed into the corner pocket using low right English. Low English will cause the cue ball to pull to the rail and back. You have to know that anytime you use low English, the cue ball will want to come back to you. The right spin on the cue ball is what will make it come back off of the rail to the second object ball.

You must get the cue ball to spin to the right in order to make this shot work. Use a moderate and smooth stroke without hitting the cue ball hard. Let the English work for you.

The second object ball will be pocketed into the left side pocket using low English to stop the cue ball.

See the diagrams below.

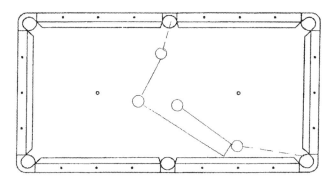

Practice Routines: Draw Shot

On these three draw shots, you're going to place the object ball different distances away from the corner pocket along with the cue ball.

You're going to pocket the object ball into the corner pocket, drawing the cue ball back to get shape on the second object ball, which is down at the other end of the table.

Your first draw shot will involve placing the object ball six inches away from the corner pocket and the cue ball twenty-four inches away from the object ball.

Your second draw shot will involve placing the object ball a little farther away from the corner pocket, twelve inches away, and the cue ball twelve inches away from the object ball.

In the third draw shot, you will place the object ball twenty-four inches from the corner pocket and the cue ball twelve inches from the object ball. With all three shots, you will draw the cue ball back and get shape on the second object ball, which is down at the other end of the table. Pocket that second object ball into the corner pocket and try to stop the cue ball, depending on the shape you get.

See diagrams below.

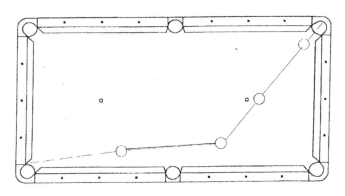

Practice Routines: Draw Shot

For this routine, pocket the first object ball into the corner pocket and draw the cue ball to the next object ball, number two. Pocket the number-two object ball also into the corner pocket, once again drawing the cue ball back to the third object ball. Pocket the third object ball into the opposite corner pocket of the table.

Place the first object ball in the middle of the table. The cue ball will be on the right side of the object ball, off the side rail one full diamond and up from the bottom rail three diamonds. Use a straight-draw English on the first object ball, using a full tip of English on the cue ball. Depending on your stroke and follow-through, you might have to use a full tip and a half of low English. Don't shoot this shot hard; use your regular stroke. It won't take much to draw the cue ball back at this angle. Make sure that you execute this shot with a smooth stroke and a good follow-through. Your follow-through should be only an inch through or past the cue ball. For the second object ball, you will use low right English—no more than a half of a tip or one full tip. The right English will bring the cue ball back to the third object ball, not the low or draw English. The low or draw English is what you need to get the cue ball to come back, not to roll forward, and to finish the shot you need the right English. The right English will spin the cue ball off the rail and bring the cue ball back and over to the third object ball.

See the diagram below.

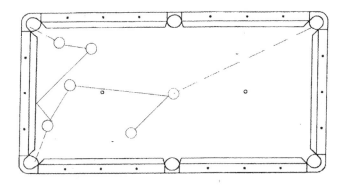

Practice Routines: Draw Shot

This practice routine will require you to use low English to draw the cue ball back to the next object ball down at the other end of the table.

The first object ball will be placed in the center of the table but up from the bottom rail one and a half diamonds.

The second object ball will be down at the other end of the table one diamond past the side pocket and up from the bottom rail three diamonds. Now from the side rail, the object ball will be one half of a diamond.

On the first object ball shot, you will be using low left English to bring the cue ball down the table for the next object ball. If you use straight low English, you will draw the cue ball almost straight back. You would still be on the upper half of the table, and that's not where you want to be. Using left English will pull the cue ball more to the left side of the object ball than if you were to use straight-draw

English, so left English on the cue ball is what is going to carry it down the table toward the object ball.

Draw Shots

If you don't get close enough to the second object ball to control the cue ball, you're out of shape. Always try to get as close to the object ball as possible.

See the diagram below.

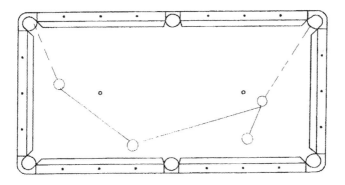

Practice Routines: Draw Shot

On this practice routine you will be using low English on the first object ball and then high English on the second object ball. Now, for the last object ball you will use low English once again.

The first object ball will be placed half a diamond up from the bottom rail. From the left side rail, you also want to be in one half of a diamond.

The second object ball will be located at the center of the table one diamond in from the right rail.

The third object ball will be located up from the bottom rail one and a half diamonds and in from the left side rail just over a diamond.

Pocket the first object ball into the corner pocket with low English, using a full tip and a half of low English on the cue ball. Make sure that your follow-through is about an inch to ensure a full draw. Also, make sure that your stroke is nice and smooth. You don't have to shoot this shot very hard; just use your normal stroke and normal speed. The follow-through will make the cue ball do what you want. If you're not drawing the cue ball back, make sure that you're using the low English that you need. Now, pull the cue ball back down the table for the next object ball.

For the second object ball use one full tip of high English above the center of the cue ball. Once again use your regular stroke—not too hard.

On the third object ball use low English and control the cue ball.

See the diagram below.

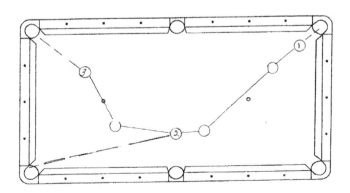

Practice Routines: Draw English

For this practice routine you will be using low left English on your first shot and then straight low English on the second and third shots.

Place the cue ball two diamonds up from the bottom rail and one diamond in from the right side rail.

The first object ball will be located up from the bottom rail three and one quarter diamonds and in from the right rail two and one quarter diamonds.

The second object ball will be down the table just past the right side pocket, in between the pocket and the first diamond and in from the right side rail one diamond.

The third object ball will be located at the other end of the table, one fourth of a diamond in from the left rail and up from the bottom rail a half of a diamond.

On the first shot, you want to make sure that you pull the cue ball to the left, toward the second object ball. Use a full tip of straight low English directly below the center of the cue ball. Along with left English, use one half of a tip to the left of the center of the cue ball. If you use straight low English without the left English, you might draw the cue ball into the side pocket. To ensure that you don't, the left English will pull the cue ball back and to the left.

Practice Routines: Draw English

On this practice routine you will use low English on the first shot. Use middle English on the second shot and low English once again on the last object ball.

The first object ball that you're going to shoot will be at the second diamond off of the right side rail and in from the right rail one half of a diamond. The cue ball will be down at the other end of the table one diamond past the side pocket nearest the right rail and in from the right rail one half of a diamond, straight in line with the first object ball.

The second object ball will be placed at the same end of the table as the first object ball but closer to the bottom rail. Place the second object ball just before the first diamond nearest the corner pocket but off of the right rail one half of a diamond.

The third object ball will be placed even with the second object ball but farther into the table, one and a half diamonds from either side rail.

Shooting the first object ball into the corner pocket requires you to use low English—one half of a tip below the center of the cue ball. This English will help slow the cue ball down so that you don't run it up the table too fast.

Shoot the second object ball into the opposite corner pocket using middle English. With English, you'll slide the cue ball over to the left of the object ball for your next shot.

For the third object ball you need to control the cue ball. If you got your shape on the third object ball, just use center English and stop the cue ball.

Make sure that you always control the cue ball even on your last shot. Never turn the cue ball loose, because that's when you get into trouble.

See the diagram below.

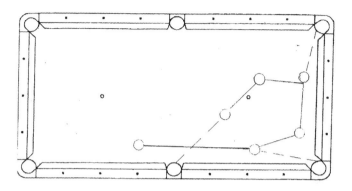

Practice Routines: Draw English

This practice routine is a bit more complicated than some of the other routines that you've already finished. You're going to be pocketing the first object ball into the corner pocket using low English or draw.

Pocket the second ball into the side pocket, using low English. The third object ball will be pocketed into the corner pocket using high English. Pocket the fourth object ball in the side pocket, using low English to draw it. Shoot the fifth object ball in the corner pocket with low English. The last object ball will be pocketed into the corner pocket using middle English on the cue ball.

Shoot the first object ball into the corner pocket with low English, one tip and a half below the center of the cue ball. You're going to draw the cue ball back about fifteen inches to get shape on your next shot. Make sure that you follow-through at least an inch past the cue ball, using a nice and smooth moderate stroke to ensure that the low English is going to work properly. You need a slight angle on the second object ball. If you have too much of an angle, you'll run the cue ball too far down the table.

Pocket the second object ball into the side pocket using low English, one full tip below the center of the cue ball. Low English will help slow the cue ball down so it won't run too far forward. Your follow-through on this shot should be about an inch through the cue ball with a moderate stroke. Make sure that the stroke is nice and smooth.

You're going to pocket the third object ball into the corner pocket. Use one full tip of high English above the center of the cue ball. Your follow-through should be no less than an inch through the cue ball with a moderate stroke to bring the cue ball around two rails. Once again make sure the stroke is nice and smooth.

Pocket the fourth object ball into the side pocket using low English to draw the cue ball back and over to the right. Use one tip of low English below the center of the cue ball using a moderate stroke. Your follow-through should be an inch through the cue ball, using one full tip and a half of low English on the cue ball.

For the fifth object ball, pocket it into the corner pocket using low English, with one tip and a half of low English. Your follow-through should be an inch through or past the cue ball. Shoot this shot with a moderate stroke to stop the cue ball.

The sixth and last object ball will be pocketed into the corner pocket using middle English with a moderate stroke to stop the cue ball.

On all of these shots, remember that you need a smooth stroke, not too hard or too soft. Most of the time, you should use a regular stroke—no more than a two on the scale from one to ten.

See the diagram below.

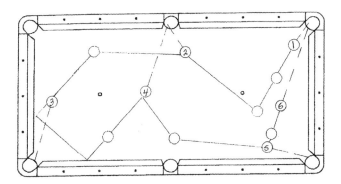

Practice Routines: Draw English

For this routine, you will be using low English on all four of the balls on the table.

The first object ball will be on the second diamond up from the bottom rail and in from the left side rail one and a half diamonds. The second ball you're going to shoot will be three diamonds up from the bottom rail and one diamond in from the right side of the table. The third ball is up from the bottom rail three diamonds and in the center of the table. Your fourth object ball will be even with the two side pockets and in from the right side rail two and a half diamonds.

On the first object ball, you will shoot in the left corner pocket using one full tip of low English below the center of the cue ball. With the angle you already have on the object ball, the cue ball will work to the right side of the table. The low English will hold the cue ball and not let it roll or run forward. When the cue ball pulls to the right, it will be on the correct side of the second object ball and in position.

On the second object ball, you will use a full tip of low English below the center of the cue ball. Slide the cue ball over to the left and in position for the third object ball.

You will shoot the third object ball using low English, one half of a tip below the center of the cue ball to hold it in position for the fourth shot.

On the fourth object ball, you need to use about a half tip of low English below the center of the cue ball to stop or hold it.

Shoot these shots with a moderate stroke and make sure it's nice and smooth.

See the diagram below.

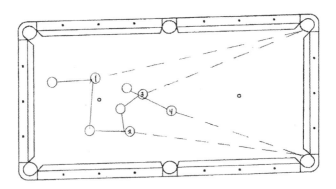

Practice Routines: Draw English

In this routine you will be using low English, high English, and then low English.

The first object ball will be placed up from the bottom rail just less than one diamond. The cue ball will be farther down the table, not quite to the side pocket on the left and in from the left side rail one diamond.

The second object ball will be at the other end of the table, one half of a diamond off the bottom rail and in from the right side rail two diamonds.

The third object ball will be at the left side pocket just off the left rail one half of a diamond and from the bottom rail three and three quarters of a diamond.

Pocket the first object ball into the corner pocket, making sure that you have a smooth stroke and a follow-through of an inch past the cue ball. Your power should be your normal stroke or speed as long as you're not hitting the cue ball too hard. Your stroke should be about a two on the scale from one to ten. You're going to be using low English, with a full tip and a half directly below the center of the cue ball, and left English one half of a tip left of the center of the cue ball. The low English will keep the cue ball from running forward, and the left English will catch the bottom rail and spin the cue ball off the rail and down to the other end of the table.

Pocket the second object ball in the corner pocket and use one full tip of high English straight above the center of the cue ball. The cue ball will come off the bottom rail and up toward the left side pocket for your last object ball.

Pocket the third object ball into the side pocket using low English, one half of a tip directly below the center of the cue ball to control it, stopping it.

See the diagram below.

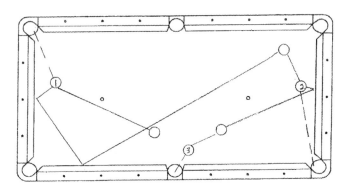

Practice Routines: Draw Shots

This practice routine starts by shooting the first object ball into the side pocket using low English. The second object ball will be pocketed into the corner pocket using low English. The third object ball is shot into the corner pocket at the other end of the table using low English again, and the fourth object ball will be shot into the corner pocket using low English once again.

Place the first object ball at the left side pocket, one half of a diamond away from the pocket in toward the table.

The cue ball will be one half of a diamond to the right of the first object ball but in the middle of the table.

Place the second object ball farther down the table off the left side rail one half of a diamond and up from the bottom rail one and one fourth diamonds.

The third object ball will be off the right side rail one half of a diamond and up from the bottom rail two and one quarter diamonds.

Pocket the first object ball into the side pocket using one full tip and a half of low English tip directly below the center of the cue ball. Use a moderate stroke with a good follow-through. You will pull the cue ball back and down the table to the second object ball, making sure that you have an angle on the second object ball.

Shoot the second object ball and use one and half tips of low English directly below the center of the cue ball. Shoot this shot with a moderate stroke—a two on the scale from one to ten. You'll be pulling the cue ball back and off of the right side rail to the third object ball.

For the third object ball, use one full tip of low English directly below the center of the cue ball. You'll be sliding the cue ball forward and to the left side of the table for the fourth object ball. You don't want to use high English because it would cause the cue ball to run forward too fast and straighten out the shot. Instead of the cue ball pulling to the left of the object ball, you could wind up right on top of the fourth object ball with no angle to make the shot. The low English will ensure you a shot on the object ball. You want to run the cue ball forward and to the left at a slow pace. That's what the low English is for.

For the fourth object ball, use low English once again to control the cue ball. Use one half of a tip directly below the center of the cue ball. Pocket the last object ball into the corner pocket.

See the diagram below.

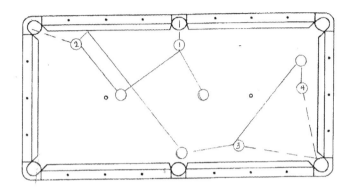

Practice Routines: Draw Shots

This is a good shot to know. It could get you out of trouble when you get straight in on the rail with the object ball.

You have two balls frozen to the bottom rail. The first ball will be the object ball, and it is one diamond away from the corner pocket. The cue ball is behind the object ball, one half of a diamond away; the two balls are not frozen together. Use low left English and pocket the object ball into the corner pocket, drawing the cue ball back to the right side rail and down the table for the next shot.

You need to pocket the object ball into the corner pocket and get shape on the next object ball, which is down at the other end of the table. It's not as hard as it looks—or is it?

Here's what is going to happen with this shot. You're going to use low left English, shooting the cue ball into the rail at a fifteen-degree angle and compressing the rail by pushing the cue ball against it and sliding the cue ball along the rail to the object ball. Make sure your followthrough is about one and one half inches past the cue ball. Shoot this shot at about a three on the scale from one to ten. Once the cue ball reaches the object ball and makes contact, the rail is going to decompress, throwing the cue ball off the rail and out to the right. Now you're drawing the cue ball to the right and not straight back. This angle will let you pull the cue ball back to the right side rail, and the left English will spin it off the side rail and down to the other end of the table for the second object ball. The left English is what is going to carry the cue ball down to the other end of the table to the next object ball.

Shoot this shot and have some fun.

See the diagram below.

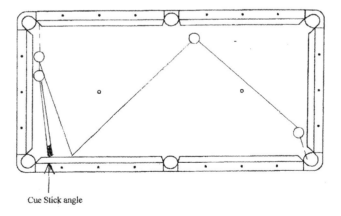

Cue Stick angle

Practice Routines: Draw Shots

This practice routine will require you to use low left English, low right English, then straight low English.

The first object ball will be placed near the spot at the center of the table, up from the bottom rail two diamonds and in from the left side rail one and a half diamonds.

The cue ball will be placed away from the right side rail one and a half diamonds in toward the object ball. From the bottom rail, the cue ball will be three and a quarter diamonds.

You will shoot the first object ball into the corner pocket. Your stroke should be a nice and smooth moderate stroke, about a two on the scale from one to ten. You will use low left English, one full tip and a half below the center of the cue ball. Your left English will be one half of a tip to the left of the center of the cue ball. You will draw the cue ball down to the other end of the table for the second object ball.

For the second object ball, you will use straight low English, one tip directly below the center of the cue ball. Your stroke should be a moderate stroke, nice and smooth. Draw the cue ball back and over to the bottom rail to the left. The cue ball will draw off the bottom rail back to the right side rail and out for position on the third object ball.

For the third object ball, use low English to control the cue ball. You don't want it to travel or go anywhere.

See the diagram below.

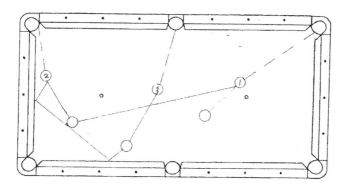

Practice Routines: Draw Shots

For this practice routine, you will be using low English.

You have two balls directly in front of the corner pocket, and you're going to pocket both balls in the same pocket, one right after the other in one shot. Using straight low English, hit the back ball straight in the center of the object ball with the cue ball, and watch both balls fall, one after the other.

What is good about this shot is that you can move the back object ball away from the second object ball an inch or two and still pocket the two balls in the same pocket. Move the back object ball several times to see how far away you can get and still pocket both balls with just one shot.

See diagram below.

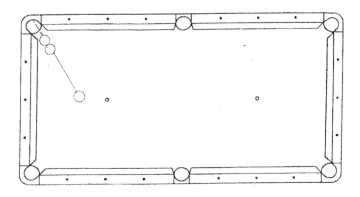

Practice Routine: Draw Shot

For this practice routine, you will be using low English. There will be two balls on the table at the end rail on your left nearest the corner pocket. The first object ball will be one half diamond away from the pocket, frozen to the left rail. The second object ball will be one half of a ball off the left rail and frozen to the first ball. With the cue ball, hit the second ball at one eighth of an inch left of center. The first ball will shoot away, and the second ball will roll forward and into the corner pocket.

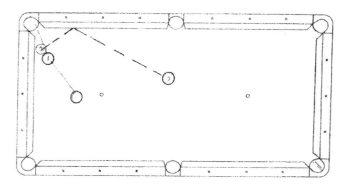

In this routine, you will be using low English.

Place the object ball on the bottom rail, frozen. The object should be close to the middle diamond. Place the cue ball on the other side of the table, one half of a diamond from the side rail and the same distance from the bottom rail. Using center low English on the cue ball, you should be able to pull or draw the cue ball back off the object ball toward the side pocket.

See the diagram below

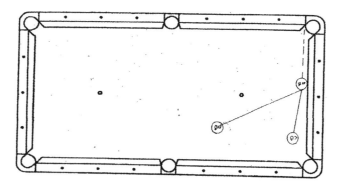

Practice Shots and Routines

In this routine, you will be using low right English.

You have two balls frozen together one diamond off the side rail in toward the center of the table and one diamond up from the bottom rail; the front ball is the object ball, and the back ball is the cue ball. The two balls are not pointed toward the pocket. They are in line with the first diamond at the other end of the table. Using low right English with a moderate stroke and a short follow-through, you're going to pocket the object ball in the left corner pocket. Aim straight at the object ball with the cue ball. This will throw the object ball toward the pocket and the cue ball off to the left. If you shoot the shot correctly, you will pocket the object ball in the left corner pocket.

See the diagram below.

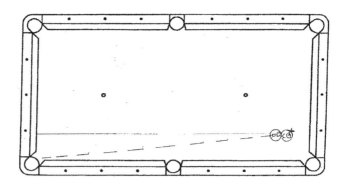

Practice Shots and Routines

In this practice routine, you will use low right English to pocket the front object ball in the side pocket.

You have two balls frozen together in the center of the table. The two balls are one half diamond from the side pocket. The cue ball will be at a forty-five-degree angle from the two object balls. Using low right English, hit the back object ball with the cue ball in the face, or a full-ball hit. The front object ball will be pulled toward the side pocket because of the friction between the two balls, therefore pocketing the front object ball in the side pocket.

See the diagram below.

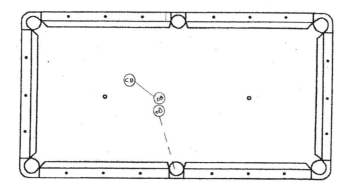

Practice Routines

In this routine, you will be using low right English.

Place the two balls just shy of the second diamond from the side pocket in the middle of the table. Make sure they are completely frozen together. The back ball will be the cue ball, and the front ball will be the object ball. Using low right English, shoot straight through the two balls with a moderate stroke and a short follow-through. If hit correctly, the object ball will spin to the left off of the cue ball, and you will pocket the object ball into the side pocket.

See the diagram below.

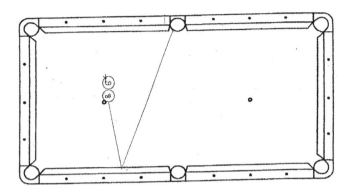

Practice Shots and Routines

In this practice routine, you're going to be using low left English to throw the object ball toward the pocket.

Place two balls on the table. The front ball of the two will be the object ball, and the back ball will be the cue ball. Now place the cue ball off the bottom rail approximately one and a half diamonds up from the bottom rail toward the center of the table. The cue ball should be off the side rail approximately one half of a diamond. Make sure that the object ball is in front of the cue ball and separated by at least one inch. Use low left English but not too much—only about a quarter of a ball. Shoot directly at the object ball with the cue ball. Use a moderate stroke with a short follow-through. This shot will throw the object ball toward the pocket.

See the diagram below.

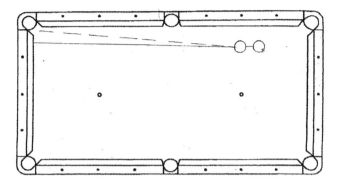

Kick Shots

The kick shot is a very simple shot if you follow the examples below.

The imaginary line that's coming off the object ball to the rail is the most important ingredient in recognizing the angle that you need to make contact or hit the object ball.

In the illustrations below, you can see an imaginary (dotted) line coming off the object ball and the path of the cue ball, where it crosses or passes through that imaginary line. Concentrate on the two darker lines after the imaginary line where the cue ball has passed through. Both of these lines must be the same length in order to make contact with the object ball.

See the diagram below.

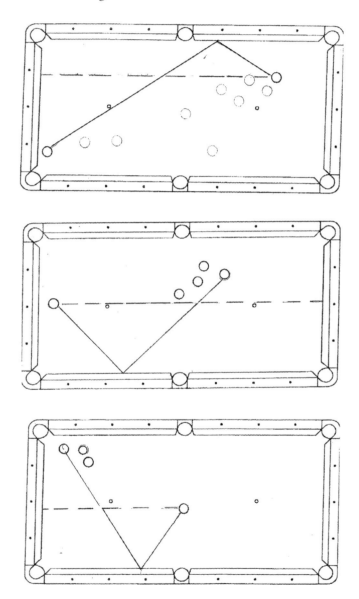

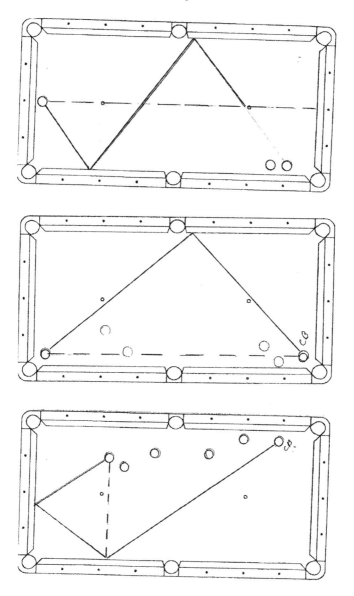

CHAPTER 3

FOCUS

Focus starts with first reading the table before you approach it. You need to get your line on the cue ball to the object ball to the pocket, determine what English you're going to use, and identify your line from the first object ball to the second object ball.

You then need to focus on getting into a good stance, staying down through the shot, staying still with no head or body movement, keeping your front hand firm, moving your arm from the elbow only, keeping the upper arm still, and then making a nice, clean, smooth stroke with good follow-through. But before all that, you need to focus on the pocket and how you decided to shoot the object ball into that pocket.

Now let's turn your focus to the hit between the cue ball and the object ball. Why? First, you need to focus on your spot on the object ball, and second, you need to see the hit between the object ball and the cue ball. This means that you've stayed down on the table without moving any part of your body. Moving would have caused you to lose focus on the object ball, and in some cases this movement can cause you to miss your spot on the object ball and therefore the shot.

Suppose you shoot the first object ball in the right side pocket so that the cue ball will carry down the table to the left side of the object ball in order to get the shape you need so you can pocket the second object ball. This is where you need that focus we described. Before you take your shot, you need to focus on the table and what English you're going to use to get to the second object ball. You can't play pool well and with consistency if your focus isn't on what you're trying to accomplish. You can make good shots, but where is the shape for the next shot? You have to be focused on each individual shot for the shape you want. Bottom line—you're taking the guesswork out of the equation.

Why guess at what you're trying to do? Don't guess. If you have the tools, use them. If you don't have the tools, then acquire them. How determined are you to learn the game of pool? How far do you really want to go with it? The game of pool can be the most invigorating sport you have ever known, or it can turn you upside down; it depends on your ability to withstand the pressure that this game can dish out. Focus—that's the name of game. Any sport that you try to master has its ups and downs, but the one thing that will increase the odds in your favor is your ability to focus. That's what sways the odds. The ability to completely focus on the task at hand and not break concentration even for one moment give you the best chance of beating your opponent.

When you do focus, what does that bring to the table? It should bring assurance and confidence. Assurance is a positive mind-set. Confidence will bring the attitude of believing in yourself and what you can accomplish when you put your mind to it. Have confidence and assurance and never look back.

The next thing to focus on would be the stroke, which consists of three mechanics: keeping your body still, keeping your head still, and most of all swinging the arm in a pendulum motion. Keeping your body still means that you've made your approach to the table, and when you're ready to start your stroke, your body is as still as possible. Your hand that's on the table holding the front of the cue stick should be set and not move in any way. If the front hand moves up or down, side to side, or in any direction, you're completely out of line with the shot. Once you make your approach to the table, you should be lined up in position to start your stroke. You need to have your English set—that's the front hand. If this hand moves, then your English will be changed. The front hand controls where the tip of the cue stick hits the cue ball.

If you want to use draw for reverse English, you have to place the tip of the cue stick at the bottom of the cue ball so that the cue ball will spin back toward you. The front hand is lowered toward the surface of the table, but if you move the front hand in any way from the low position of the cue ball for draw English, you will change the English to something else. If you move the front hand up, you will have middle English; and if you move your hand up a lot, you will have high English. The cue ball's reaction will be to run forward instead of drawing back. All of this depends on focus.

Keep focused and play your best pool.

CHAPTER 4

EQUIPMENT

First of all, do you know how to maintain your equipment? I'm talking about the shaft of the cue stick.

Your local billiard store has a cleaner for cue sticks. If you don't want to buy a special cleaner and your shaft is made out of wood, you can use window cleaner. I prefer Windex window cleaner. Spray the shaft with Windex, or wet a soft, clean cloth or towel with it. With the towel in your hand, hold the cue stick and wipe the whole shaft vigorously from top to bottom. This will remove a lot of the chalk and other residue that may have built up. Make sure that you dry the shaft completely right away; never leave it damp. The shaft should be warm if it is completely dry. After it is dry, 400-grit sandpaper to start. Sand the whole shaft, pressing lightly and spinning the shaft as you go. Then use 600-grit sandpaper until the shaft is nice and smooth. Wipe it with a dry, clean, smooth towel.

What's in your pool case besides your cue stick, your break stick, and maybe a jump cue? These are some of the things that you really need to carry: extra tips, a tip replacement kit, 320-grit sandpaper to clean the cue stick tip for tip replacement, extra chalk, a tip pick, and a rasp to shape the tip.

CHAPTER 5

THE APPROACH TO THE TABLE

The first step in approaching the table is standing at a forty-five degree angle to the table. Place the cue ball about two feet out from the bottom rail and the same distance from the side rail, two feet out on your right. Make sure that the cue ball is right in front of you where you can easily reach it with the tip of the cue stick. Hold the cue stick in the hand you would normally use to grip and stroke the cue stick. Now rest the cue stick in your hand in a cradling position, with four fingers underneath it and the thumb over the top (not on top of the cue stick but *over* the top), gripping the cue stick loosely. Hold the cue stick in the middle of the wrap. Place the cue stick on the rail of the table with the cue stick tip no more than one half of an inch from the cue ball.

(I will give directions specifically for right-handed people, but if you are left handed, please just reverse the specified hand.) With your right hand, hold the cue in the middle of the wrap, place your right hand with the cue stick on your hip, and bend the elbow slightly so that the tip of the cue stick is on the surface of the table. Keep the right foot firmly on the floor. The right foot is your foundation. Now relax, with most of your weight on the right leg. Place the left foot or leg slightly in front of the right foot or leg, about a foot or so, in a normal standing posture.

Now place an object ball on the table approximately two feet in front of the cue ball and repeat the process, but this time try to line up with the object ball. To do so, place the cue stick on the table one half inch away from the center of cue ball. Point the cue stick through the cue ball by looking down the shaft to the object ball. When you have your line, remember that the back leg is your foundation; that leg should be firmly planted. Now all you need to do is step forward with the left front leg, bend at the knee, and slide your left hand under the cue stick shaft all the way up toward the cue ball until your hand is approximately six inches from the end of the cue stick. Raise the front hand, and you should be ready to make the shot. The back foot should not be moved during this process. If you move the back leg after it is in position, you have moved your whole body and gotten out of position. You would need to start all over. Once you have your line and a good foundation, don't move your leg. Now with the cue stick on your hip and the tip of the cue stick at the base of the cue ball one half inch away from the cue ball, step forward enough to where you are bent over at the waist and stretched out to where the front hand is roughly six inches away from the end of the cue stick. Raise the front hand so the cue stick tip is in the middle of the cue ball and make the shot. Repeat the process until you are comfortable.

CHAPTER 6

MOVEMENT

The next thing we want to be aware of and focus on is your bodily movement. First, let's discuss the importance of setting up and then not moving the back foot. The back foot is your foundation on the lower half of the body. You want to keep your body as still as possible.

Next, think about your front hand, which we discussed briefly earlier. This hand is the one that will be on the table holding the cue stick and is your foundation for the position on the cue ball and the English you intend to use. You shouldn't worry about the tip of the cue stick being off your mark on the cue ball if you haven't moved your front hand. Your hand is still in the same position that it was when you got your line, so if you haven't moved your hand, your positioning on the cue ball is still solid.

When you have a good foundation from the back leg up to the hand that's on the table, where do you go next?

A complete lack of head movement is so important. There should be no head movement. If the head is not still but moving from one side to the other or up and down before the shot, then you have body movement. When you move the head, you move the whole body. And that body movement causes you to lack focus or concentration on your line to the object ball and from the cue ball.

One last thing is eye movement. When you look away from the object ball, you lose your line or focus. When you move your eyes, you move your head slightly. Looking at the cue ball once too often causes you to lose your line to the object ball. Moving your eyes causes you to lose sight or clarity of your line on the cue ball. The same goes for the object ball, and then you won't have a clear line of sight on either ball. How many times should you look at the cue ball? *Once!* Why should you look at the cue ball more than once? When you do, you're telling yourself that you're not sure if you're still on the spot on the cue ball that you need to make the shot. If you haven't moved the front hand, you're good. Don't second guess yourself about your position on the cue ball with the tip of the cue stick. When you look at the cue ball more than once, you lose focus on the intended line or your spot on the cue ball, which is lined up with the object ball. The spot on the cue ball should be clear and not blurred in any way. Moving the eyes back and forth to the cue ball and then back to the object ball and back again blurs your vision or focus. Why should you want to blur your vision on the object ball or the cue ball? The object ball is the one you want to hit perfectly with the cue ball. So if you glance back and forth from the cue ball to the object ball, you're going to lose focus. Until you get comfortable getting your line on the cue ball and transferring your focus to the object ball, don't look down to the cue ball more than once. Lining up should become second nature with practice. You're already lined up when you make your approach to the table, so why should you have to check again and again to see if you're still in line with your shot? Your focus should be simultaneously on *the cue ball, the object ball, and the intended pocket* when you approach the table, all at a glance. That's the focus you should be striving to achieve.

The prestroke is stroking the cue stick in rhythm just before you take the shot. When you do this, don't break your focus on the object ball. Don't force yourself to take the shot until you feel relaxed and comfortable. Get your line, focus on the object ball, and take a deep breath. Make a smooth stroke and pocket the object ball. Make this a routine. Set up a good foundation on the back foot and the front hand while looking at the object ball, and with a smooth stroke once again, pocket the object ball.

CHAPTER 7

THE LINE TO THE OBJECT BALL

Let's look at how to line up with the center of the cue ball to the center of the object ball. Then we'll discuss how to line up the object ball with the pocket. Place an object ball on the table by the side pocket approximately one foot away from the pocket itself toward the middle of the table. Place the cue ball on the opposite side of the table two feet from the side pocket and in line with the object ball toward the center of the table. You want to be able to pocket the object ball into the side pocket. Your first focus should be your approach to the table. You should be one half inch from the center of the cue ball with the tip of the cue stick resting on the table. The cue stick should be pointed toward the object ball. Now your second focus should be to look down the shaft of the cue stick still pointing to the center of the cue ball. Follow the line of the cue stick shaft to the center of the object ball, through the object ball, and to the pocket. Every time you get your line on the center of the cue ball, you should be lining up directly with the object ball toward the pocket where you plan to pocket the object ball. Now pocket the object ball. Do the same setup (pocket the object ball into the side pocket) until you're comfortable with that shot. Now this time, place the object ball back onto the table; rotate the cue ball over one quarter of a turn to the right or left, whichever you prefer; and pocket the object ball in the same side pocket. Repeat the same drill until you have successfully rotated the cue ball four quarters of a turn for four different angles of position. Do the same shot with the other five pockets until you have used all six pockets on the pool table successfully.

CHAPTER 8

STROKE

What do you know about the stroke? The amateur's stroke involves holding the cue stick in the right or left hand and swinging it back and forth at the cue ball. Then, the stick hits the cue ball, sometimes as hard as possible. Most amateurs, or beginners, just learning to play the game have a lot of fun, but they don't really have any technique, which is a large part of the stroke. Whether you're a pro or a beginner, the stroke is one of the most important parts of your game. If you don't have a decent stroke, those shots that you've been missing could be the result of your stroke not being as smooth and consistent as it should be. The stroke is the weapon that will carry you through game after game with a steady flow of excellence, not faltering under the pressure of your opponent. Your stroke should be as steady as a surgeon's hand—a steady flow of excellence, smooth and consistent time after time. Do you know the difference between an amateur and a pro? The pro has a smooth stroke, and the key is the smoothness with which he or she comes through the stroke.

The stroke consists of a pendulum motion, an arm movement from the elbow down to the hand. The upper portion of the arm is kept motionless as much as possible. Now the motion that you strive for in the stroke is the swaying motion, once again of that pendulum swaying back and forth in a smooth, repetitious movement. The beginning of the stroke is the pendulum stroking the cue stick in a smooth manner, first away from the cue ball back to front and then back to front again and again until you feel that you are ready to finish the shot, with the last stroke being just the follow-through and then pocketing the object ball. The back-to-front motion should be as smooth as possible. It is the part of the stroke where you can lose the smoothness. How do you achieve that motion or smoothness? Most players use a very rapid and jerky motion when they pull away from the cue ball, forcing the stroke forward. This jerky motion is what causes you to miss the mark on the cue ball where you have lined up. You have to smooth out that jerky movement of the back-to-front stroke. As you're getting into the stroke, pause a little longer than normal just as you pull the cue stick away from the cue ball. The pause should be very slight, almost a nonmovement, to where you *slowly* pull away and *slowly* pick up the speed of the cue stick to the back of the stroke. The forward motion should not begin by just bringing the cue stick forward in a natural movement. The movement should not be rapidly pulling or forcing the cue stick forward. When you start the forward stroke, you should once again pause as you normally would, but then start the forward motion *slower* than usual. Then slowly and smoothly pick up your speed or slowly accelerate to the speed you need. Do these exercises every time you start the forward stroke and also the stroke coming back away from the cue ball by pausing that extra little bit. This will allow you to bring your stroke up to speed at a slower acceleration and help you achieve that smoother stroke you desire.

If you have a stroke like Alison Fisher, where you stop the stroke completely at the cue ball, start the backswing or stroke by slowly accelerating away from the cue ball. Accelerating too fast will move your whole body, and that will take away the smoothness and the steadiness of the stroke that you're trying to achieve. Moving the body out of control, or uncontrollable, not on purpose means that you are not in control of your stroke. Moving the stroke too quickly from back to front and front to back causes the stroke to move the body; therefore, the stroke has no consistency. If your body moves from side to side, where does the cue stick move? Does the cue stick move with your body? Why, yes! Your cue stick will follow your body's movement. So when you move just a little to the left or just a little to the right on the backward stroke or the motion coming forward, your cue stick will follow that movement. When the cue stick moves left or right, your stroke will be off to the left or right, which would mean that the line you had on the cue ball is now left or right of your line on the object ball also. By moving, you could miss the cue ball, or more likely you're probably going to miss the shot on the object ball.

Do we understand body movement and why it's so crucial to the stroke? How can we improve body movement or get it under control? Body movement is the result of the stroke being forced forward or backward too fast. When you're standing with both feet flat on the ground, move your arms out in front of you, straight away from your body. What does your body do? How does your body react? Your body will compensate for the movement by moving the rest of the body backward. If the body doesn't move backward, then you'll fall forward. If you move your arms backward, the rest of the body will move forward to compensate for the movement. When you force the cue stick or stroke forward or backward in a rapid movement, this will cause your body to react in the same rapid movement. The body will move and compensate for the rapid movement of the stroke, and this causes the body to move uncontrollably. So when the stroke is out of control and the body is out of control, what will the results be? Miscue, miss your spot on the object ball, failure to pocket the ball, and miss the intended mark on where you needed to hit the cue ball. These are some of the results of a bad and inconsistent stroke. If you wonder why you miss a lot of shots and why you can't pocket balls consistently, start by checking your stroke. Is your stroke out of control? Every good athlete has a controlled swing, hit, punch, or throw that they control. They start slowly into motion and then accelerate through. The result is control. If you control the movement of your stroke in a smooth and controlled manner, the body will also move in a smooth and controlled manner. Now what do you think the percentage might be on making the shot if you have control over your stroke?

CHAPTER 9

HIGH ENGLISH

There are three basic English shots. We have to underline *basic*. There are high English, middle English, and low English. Now before we get started, let's think of what those three types of English will do when used properly. All English action and reaction will occur after the cue ball makes contact with the object ball. High English will send the cue ball forward and to the rail quickly. Middle English will stop the cue ball from rolling forward or backward at a short distance and will also send it to the side in a straight line. Low English will draw the cue ball back in a reverse motion or, if needed, just slow it down when used properly or even stop it at long range. With this in mind, let's get started.

Using our setup from an earlier chapter, "The Line to the Object Ball," set the object ball in the same position at the side pocket, about one foot in front of the pocket toward the middle of the table. Place the cue ball on the opposite side of the table out in front of the pocket also toward the middle of the table about two feet instead of one foot. When you approach the table while cradling the cue stick in your hand, place your cue stick tip on the table at the bottom of the cue ball one half inch away from the cue ball. Your line should be once again with the cue stick at the center of the bottom of the cue ball along with the center of the object ball. Slide your front hand under the cue stick shaft and lean forward onto the table, bending at the waist with a strong foundation at the front hand. You should raise the front hand slightly in an upward motion, raising the cue stick tip toward the top of the cue ball about one full tip up from the center of the cue ball. Make sure that you keep the cue stick level with the butt of the cue stick just up off the rail of the table. Only the front hand should be raised or moved in the direction of the English you're using. In other words, the front hand, when placed on the table, should move in the position of your English—up, down, or side to side.

For high English, your front hand should be raised so that your cue stick will be not quite at the top of the cue ball—flat with the table for "draw English" (low English), and for stop English or middle English, your hand should be only slightly raised so the tip of the cue stick tip is at the center or in the middle of the cue ball. Once you have the proper height for the high English, make sure that the front hand doesn't move. The front hand should be your solid foundation, not to be moved but kept very still with no movement. Any movement of the front hand will cause you to miss your mark on the cue ball, and this in turn will most likely cause you to miss the object ball on one side or the other. Now the English that you're striking the cue ball with will be high English, which will start the cue ball spinning forward as it leaves the tip of the cue stick. This will cause the cue ball to make contact with the object ball and then keep traveling forward. With the object ball at the side pocket and the cue ball on the opposite side of the table, stroke the cue stick at least three times as smoothly as possible as to get your motion or, as they say, your prestroke. Now on the last stroke, strike the cue ball with high English (one full tip above the center of the cue ball) with a short follow-through of about one inch and pocket the object ball. Did the cue ball travel forward? If not, make sure you're still on the high side of the cue ball and try the same shot again. Shoot this shot until you notice that the cue ball is traveling forward after contacting the object ball. With the cue ball and the object ball back on the table this time, place the two balls just a little closer together, with the cue ball in the center of the table straight across from the object ball. The object ball will be in the same position on the table as before, or just about five or six inches out from the pocket. Shoot this shot again until the cue ball runs forward even a little. Then increase your follow-through just a little, and you should notice that the cue ball will run a little further than before. Practice this as many times as possible to get the action you desire.

High Right English

Let's put the high English and right English together. High English of course will run the cue ball forward after you make contact with the object ball.

What affect will right English have on the cue ball after it makes contact with the object ball? Let's set up the cue ball and the object ball on the table to find out. Place the cue ball about twelve inches out from the side pocket toward the middle of the table. Place the object ball across the table from the cue ball only six inches from the other side pocket. Now you're going to pocket the object ball into the side pocket, but of course you're also going to use right English along with high. Use about a full tip above the center of the cue ball of high English. Now with the right English use a half of a tip off to the right of the cue ball. You're going to shoot the cue ball at the center of the object ball and pocket the ball. Use a moderate stroke for the shot. The amount of right English you use will determine how much the cue ball will pull or spin off center. Right now we're only using a half of a tip to the right, so the cue ball won't pull or veer off to the right that much and should just clear the side pocket to the right. Just remember that when you apply right English to the cue ball, it will start rotating slightly to the right. This rotation will cause the cue ball to grab the nap or cloth of the table and start pulling the cue ball off center to the right portion of the object ball. So we're aiming at the center of the object ball. The cue ball won't hit the center of the object ball because of the right English; the English will pull the cue ball off to the right. So high English will run the cue ball forward after making contact with the object ball and Right English will cause the cue ball to run to the rail, spin off the rail, and run slightly to the right of the pocket and down toward the bottom rail. If you used just high English, the cue ball would run forward and straight into the side pocket a long with the object ball. The rotation of the right English threw the cue ball off to the right of the object ball, therefore missing the scratch in the side pocket. Shoot this shot as many times as it takes to get comfortable with it.

High Left

We covered in a previous chapter high right English, and now we will discuss high left. You should use a moderate stroke for this shot. The same movement as high right still applies to the cue ball, except the movement will be the opposite. When struck with high right English, the cue ball will first move to the left. So, when struck on the left side, the cue ball will first push the cue ball to the right. How do we or can we prove this theory? Let's place the cue ball at one end of the table out from the corner pocket at the first diamond off the bottom rail two ball lengths off the rail. Place the cue ball across the table about two feet out from the side rail. Get your line where you would with a normal shot and at normal speed. Now pocket the object ball a few times to get your speed of the cue stick and the left English to work the way you want and you're comfortable with the shot. Now your setup should be the same as before, just like you're going to make the object ball once again with your normal stroke and normal speed of the cue stick, but this time you're going to shoot the cue ball twice the speed as before. When you do this, the cue ball will stay out to the right longer than before (since your speed is faster), which means it will not hit the spot on the object ball where you were aiming. The cue ball is going to hit the object ball farther to the right of the ball proving the theory. At normal speed you make the object ball, and with your speed increased, this is what has happened; you have failed to pocket the object ball. If you have an angle—say, a quarter of aa inch—on the object ball where you need to hit the ball to pocket it, shoot the cue ball as a normal shot then after you have pocketed the object ball several times repeat the process. Speed up your stroke a little more and see if you miss the mark on the object ball. Ok let's take a step further, place the object ball in the middle of the table between the two side pockets of the table. Place the cue ball one foot to the left of the object ball and down toward the bottom rail and back away from the object ball about three feet. So now you're two feet to the left side and three feet from the object ball away. What I want you to do is pocket the object ball in the side pocket with a normal stroke and speed. After you have pocketed the object ball several times and have your spot on it where you know for sure that you're going to pocket it with no problem, pick up your speed by about double and aim at the same spot on the object ball and pocket the ball. You need plenty of speed on the cue ball. If you didn't pocket the ball, how close did you come to the pocket with the shot? If you had enough speed, you shouldn't have pocketed the ball. That's how much the cue ball stays out to one side or the other depending on which side of the cue ball you're using your English. This is something you really need to remember for further reference. You need to be aware of the speed you're using to pocket any ball. Speed is so important, so keep this in mind. When you add a little more speed than you would normally use on the cue ball, just remember to allow for the throw (movement) of the cue ball. Practice using different variations of speed on the cue ball until you get used to the throw (movement) of the cue ball. So use some speed on the cue ball and see how it reacts to the speed that you apply. Practice and practice until you get comfortable with this shot.

CHAPTER 10

MIDDLE ENGLISH

Now let's try to use middle English. This will be what they call a stop shot. Let's set the scene. Place the object ball in front of the side pocket on either side about one foot away from the pocket toward the center of the table. Place the cue ball in front of the object ball toward the center of the table about two feet away from the object ball. Now for the bridge hand. Place your hand under the cue stick, sliding forward and raising the cue stick slightly with the bridge hand or front hand to allow the cue stick tip to be at the middle of the cue ball. The middle English, if applied correctly, will allow the cue ball to slide all the way to the object ball and cause the cue ball to stop on contact, with no forward motion or backward motion. If the cue ball doesn't stop, you probably need to slightly increase the speed of the cue stick to make sure that the cue ball slides just a little more before making contact with the object ball. If the cue ball is rolling forward, as in a high English shot, check two things. Make sure that you're not raising the cue stick tip by pushing the butt of the cue stick downward, and make sure that you have enough speed and follow-through. Ensure that you keep the cue stick tip in the center of the cue ball. If you raise the tip in any way, then the shot becomes a high English shot, so check the position of the cue stick tip to make sure your English is correct. If, once again, the cue ball doesn't stop on contact with the object ball but rolls forward, once again make sure you have enough follow-through along with sufficient speed of the cue stick to slide the cue ball all the way to the object ball. What is happening when the cue ball doesn't stop but rolls forward after the cue ball has made contact with the object ball is that the cue ball has already started to roll forward just *before* the cue ball reaches the object ball. Anytime the cue ball starts to roll forward *before contact,* the cue ball wants to continue to roll forward. You have used high English. You may have shot the cue ball too soft and with insufficient speed. The cue ball must be shot hard enough with a smooth stroke so that it can slide all the way to the object ball. The sliding motion ensures that when the cue ball comes in contact with the object ball, the cue ball will stop because there is no forward motion. Another thing that would cause the cue ball to continue to run forward after contact is you may have dropped or lowered the back (butt) of the cue stick. You may have forced your elbow downward, causing the cue stick tip to raise up just a little and therefore causing the high English to take place.

Let's check where the tip of the cue stick should be after the shot. It should be down on the table, meaning that you had a perfect stroke and follow-through. If the tip of the cue stick is not down on the pool table, this means that you have once again raised the tip of the cue stick and caused the cue ball to run forward. Shoot this shot until you have stopped the cue ball on contact with good speed and follow-through and the tip of the cue stick is on the pool table after the shot. If the cue ball stops on contact, you have successfully shot a middle English shot or stop shot.

CHAPTER 11

LOW ENGLISH

What are some of the things that we know about low English? We know that it will draw the cue ball back to us. We can also stop the cue ball from running forward by using low English. We know that if you don't want the cue ball to run to the rail too fast, you can use low English to slow it down. You can also pull the cue ball left or right using low English.

There are several other types of English that you can apply to the cue ball to make it act and react to what you want it to do. For instance, if you want the cue ball to run forward but not too fast, use low English.

Let's get into using low English. Let's say you want to run the cue ball left of the pocket while still aiming at the center of the pocket and centered with the object ball. Now you need some distance between the cue ball and the object ball. Place the object ball about five inches out from the side pocket out toward the middle of the table and the cue ball on the opposite side of the table out from the pocket toward the middle of the table about twelve inches from the pocket.

Now you're going to line up directly in line or toward the object ball, but with the cue stick tip you want to be just to the left side of the cue ball. Your cue stick tip should be one full tip low and one half of a tip left of the center of the cue ball. Now you have to use a moderate stroke, nothing too hard; you have to let the English work. Hitting left of center of the cue ball means that when you follow through with the last stroke of the cue stick to the cue ball, the cue ball will start to rotate to the left just a little. This motion of the cue ball will start to pull the cue ball off to the left of the center of the object ball. You're still going to pocket the object ball, but now you're throwing low left English on the cue ball, just enough to pull the cue ball off line or off center of the object ball. The cue ball then will or should still run forward with the English, but because of the left English on the cue ball, it will pull toward the left, still making contact with the object ball but on the left side, pocketing the object ball into the pocket on the right corner of the pocket. The cue ball should then run to the rail just to the left of the pocket. Everything should run to the left because of the position of the cue stick tip on the cue ball, which was *left*. The same applies when you use right English: the cue ball will run to the right of the object ball.

Let's take it one step at a time. The first step is low English, which is also called draw English. Draw English will cause the cue ball to spin backward and therefore come back toward you or return to you. Place the cue ball and the object ball on the table. The object ball will be placed about one foot out from the side pocket toward the center of the table. The cue ball should be placed on the opposite side of the table about one foot away from the object ball. The way we have been approaching the table never changes. Start by lining up the shot with the cue ball directly in line with the object ball. You're going to pocket the object ball into the side pocket. Now establish a good foundation, which is of course your back leg and foot firmly on the floor. Bend at the waist and step forward with the left foot, if you are right handed (or right foot if you are left handed). Don't move the foundation foot or you will lose your line. Slide the front hand under the shaft of the cue stick and run your hand to the table toward the cue ball, stopping about six inches from the end of the cue stick. Position the front hand on the table with the cue stick tip at the bottom of the cue ball. The tip of the cue stick should be approximately one half of an inch away from the cue ball. Lower the front hand until the cue stick tip is at the bottom of the cue ball. Now we need the cue stick tip to be not in the center of the cue ball but one full tip below the center of the cue ball. Now you want to stroke the cue stick at least three times; this is your prestroke. On the final stroke, *do not increase the speed of the cue stick toward the cue ball just before you hit the cue ball.* Just follow through about an inch with your last stroke and pocket the object ball. If the shot has been executed correctly, the cue ball should have returned or rolled back toward you. If the cue ball stops after the object ball has been struck with the cue ball, you may have brought the cue stick tip up by dropping the butt of the cue stick or raised the front hand slightly more toward the center of the cue ball instead of toward the bottom. These two things will cause you to hit more in the center of the cue ball and not at the bottom.

One way to make sure that you are using low English is to see where the tip of the cue stick is located after the shot. Is it on the table, or is it in the air and off the table? If it is off the table, you have probably lowered the butt of the cue stick and therefore raised the tip, hitting the center of the cue ball rather than the lower part and causing the shot to be a stop shot rather than a draw shot. This time, freeze after the shot; don't move. Look and make sure that the cue stick tip is on the table after the shot, not up in the air. This will give you some indication that you're performing the shot correctly. You'll have better results with this shot if you check after every shot until you get comfortable with it.

Low English can also stop the cue ball if your next shot is too far down the table to use a middle-English shot to stop the cue ball. How do we accomplish that? Let's put the shot in perspective. Low English will draw the cue ball back toward you, correct? How does that happen? Well, the cue ball spins in a reverse motion, so after the cue ball makes contact with the object ball, the cue ball is still spinning in the backward motion and so it comes back. When you shoot the same shot but from farther away—say, about three feet farther—the cue ball will spin in a normal fashion but then slow down to about half the spin it needs to return toward you. Check it out. Shoot the shot and see what the results might be. If it only comes back a little, let's lengthen the shot even farther, to five feet. Once again, use the same amount of spin and follow through as when you shot the first shot. With the same amount of English, shoot the shot once again and see what happens. Did the cue ball stop? If yes, why did it stop instead of coming back toward you? The cue ball was rotating with an underspin when the object ball was closer, therefore when the cue ball made contact with the object ball while the cue ball was still spinning in reverse, the cue ball returned toward you. So when you lengthened the shot, used the same amount of underspin, and the cue ball made contact with the object ball, this time the cue ball was no longer spinning in a backward or reverse motion or rotating forward, if the length of the shot was correct. You might have to lengthen the distance between the cue ball and the object ball, or maybe even shorten the distance. If your distance is correct, the cue ball should actually just start to slide when the cue ball comes in contact with the object ball, therefore stopping the cue ball. Now if the cue ball rolled forward just a little, move the object ball just a little closer so it is not quite so far away. Keep making little adjustments until you have the right distance for the cue ball to come to a stop. Practice this shot until you are comfortable.

Now to run the cue ball forward just a little with low English. Say you're about three feet away from the object ball that you're going to pocket. You don't want the cue ball to run to a rail because the next object ball is in between two other balls and you only need to run the cue ball four inches to get shape for the shot. If applied correctly, you can use low English to run the cue ball two inches or six feet. If you're three feet away from the object ball you're going to pocket and the cue ball needs to run only four inches, use three quarters of a tip of low English below the center of the cue ball with a moderate stroke and see if the cue ball rolls too far forward or gives you the results you are looking for. If the cue ball draws back, then use one half of a tip of low English with the same stroke; don't change your stroke. If you change your stroke, then you will have changed the whole shot. Always use the same stroke with just about every shot, and let your English control the shot.

Now what about pulling the cue ball left or right after making contact with the object ball for your next shot with low English? If you're lined up straight in or off to one side of the pocket, you can still pull the cue ball to either side of the pocket after contact with the object ball using low English. Place the object ball one foot from the side pocket and the cue ball across from the object ball straight into the pocket about two feet away. Here's what we do. Line the object ball up with the center of the pocket, and do the same with the cue ball. You're going to use low right English if you want the cue ball to pull to the right off the object ball. The first thing that happens with the cue ball is that the English on the right side will push the cue ball slightly to the left coming off the cue stick. Then the cue ball will pull to the right because of the rotation or right spin you just applied to the cue ball. Your right English on the cue ball pulls hard to the right mainly because of the low English. You're pulling the cue ball back toward you, but because of the right English on the cue ball you have now thrown the cue ball off line or off center of the object ball and therefore the cue ball will now drift to the right. Now the farther away from the object ball you are, the more the cue ball will pull to the right. Use the same English at the bottom left on the cue ball for the same results to the left. Practice this shot and get comfortable it. Then lengthen the shot another five to six inches using the same English and see the results.

Low Left

One thing we need to understand about left English is that when we apply it, there is an opposite reaction of the cue ball. The cue ball will first travel a short distance to the right depending on how much force you apply to the cue ball. The force will determine how long the cue ball stays out to the right. You might not notice the cue ball's movement to the right, but that's the reaction you need to expect. When you hit the cue ball to the left, you're actually pushing it to the right first. Then the cue ball of course will start to work back to the left for the intended shot. One other thing you need to know is that the softer you hit or stroke the cue ball, the less reaction to the right you will get on the cue ball. It will be pushed to the right only a little and react faster to the left English, pulling back to the left very quickly. The harder you hit the cue ball, the farther it will travel to the right and the longer it will stay to the right before starting to work back to the left. So hitting the cue ball with a hard stroke using left English will cause the cue ball to stay out to the right longer, which means a slower reaction time on the cue ball to come back to the intended shot or to the left.

Now make sure that you have a small angle with this shot, or you can create the angle you need by cheating the pocket to the right. You know that low English is draw English, which will pull the cue ball back in your direction. Left English will cause you to throw or drift the cue ball left of the object ball before and after contact. Use a moderate stroke for this shot. For instance, we're going to change it up a little to give you an idea of how the left English will work. If you use middle left English on the cue ball, the cue ball will start to rotate like a top in a left spinning motion. So when the cue ball makes contact with the object ball, the cue ball will slide just a little forward, if any at all, depending on how hard or soft you shoot or stroke the cue ball. The cue ball should come off the object ball in a straight line to the left because you haven't put any low English on the cue ball yet. Remember your angle. In this shot use about a full tip below the center of the cue ball of low English. Use one quarter of a tip with the left English. You know how the cue ball will react to the left English—the English will slide or throw the cue ball left. Now, low English on the cue ball will most likely draw or stall the cue ball depending on how much you follow through on the cue ball. You want a short follow through. Using a moderate stroke, let's put both low English and left English together. Now it depends on how far you want the cue ball to run or drift left. If you want the cue ball to run a little farther to the left, you need to use more left English, and maybe you could hit the cue ball just a little softer or sometimes a little harder. If you need the cue ball to come back just a little more, of course use a little more of the low English, maybe another quarter of a tip lower on the cue ball. If the cue ball drew too much, come up one quarter of a tip on your draw English. Shoot this shot until the cue ball reacts to the English you're using and you have the cue ball under control. You may have to put in a considerable amount of time to get the cue ball under control, but it will be worth the effort.

Low Right

When using low right English, use the same method as you would with the low left, knowing that the cue ball will act and react the same but in the opposite direction of low left English.

First, let's start by setting up low English. Put the cue stick in the middle of the cue ball, then lower the tip of the cue stick one full tip toward the bottom of the cue ball. Now for the right English. Place the tip of the cue stick in the center of the cue ball and then one full tip toward the bottom of the cue ball just as before now slide the cue stick tip over to the right of the cue ball about one half of a tip. Now the cue stick is at the bottom of the cue ball one full tip and over to the right one half of a tip. First of all, what you're going to experience is the cue ball moving to the left. But the cue ball won't move to the left as much as it would if you were shooting it using high English. One of the reasons that the cue ball won't move as much is that the low English slows the cue ball down, not releasing the cue ball and letting it travel. When the cue ball travels, it has more velocity than it does with low English. So there is less push on the cue ball side to side, and that means less travel and of course a faster or quicker action and reaction time on the cue ball. In other words, the cue ball is going to start to move in the intended direction quicker than you would expect.

CHAPTER 12

RIGHT ENGLISH

Besides the basic three types of English—high, middle, and low—there are so many other variations that will go along with them, but they are somewhat modified. You will still use the three basics but with a little tweak.

How do we apply right English to the cue ball? The first thing we need to understand is that when right English is applied, the cue ball will react to the right-hand push of the cue stick and therefore move first to the left before coming back and traveling to the right. The harder you push or hit the cue ball to the right will determine the length of time and distance the cue ball will stay out to the left. The slower you stroke or the softer you hit the cue ball, the faster the recovery time of the cue ball to the right will be. If you hit it softly and slowly, the cue ball will move to the left just a fraction of an inch and recover quickly. Now we're going to start using right English.

We're going to be using the center of the cue ball. Right English consists of pushing or stroking the cue ball to the right side of the center of the cue ball using one half of a tip to the right with a moderate stroke to start the cue ball rotating to the right. To give you an idea of the spin on the cue ball we're talking about, let's say you shoot (stroke) the cue ball the length of the table using a moderate stroke with not much speed and right English, just a half of a tip to the right. The minute you strike the cue ball, you'll notice that it will start to rotate just a little with a right-hand spin. Now place the cue ball on the table in the middle of the bottom rail about one foot off the rail and aim the cue ball toward the other rail at the other end of the table at the center diamond of that rail. Using a half of a tip of right English just off the center of the cue ball, shoot the cue ball to the other rail. Now watch where the cue ball hits the rail. Did it hit where you were aiming—at the center? The answer should be no. If you used right English with a half tip to the right and used a moderate stroke, you should have hit the other rail not at the center but just off to the right of the center of that rail. Now if you use more than half of a tip of right English, you will increase the angle to the right. In other words, the cue ball will work over to the right more than it did with the first shot. The angle will be greater than before (more to the right) because you pushed the cue ball more to the right, creating more spin on the cue ball. Therefore, the cue ball will grab the table and will work harder pulling to the right.

Place the cue ball on the table one foot out from the side pocket toward the center of the table. Place the object ball across the table out from that side pocket about six inches toward the center of the table. You're going to shoot the cue ball with one half of a tip of right English, aiming at the center of the object ball. Use a soft moderate stroke, about a two on a scale of one to ten. When you shoot the cue ball, watch what your English is going to do as the cue ball runs toward the center of the object ball. When about halfway to the object ball, the cue ball should start to rotate toward the right side of the object ball, but you should still pocket the object ball. The object ball will be pocketed in the left side of the pocket because of the right English. The cue ball will hit the right side of the object ball because of the right English, and it will travel forward and hit the rail just a little to the right of the pocket.

CHAPTER 13

MASSÉ SHOT

Short Massé

Use a high angle of the cue stick if you have a shot where you need to curve the cue ball around another ball or a jump shot but are not going to use a jump cue, just your normal cue stick. For now, forget the jump shot and concentrate on the massé shot. To start off, place the cue ball at the middle diamond about three fourths of a diamond out from the left short rail at the end of the table. Set one object ball, which we'll call the blocker, on the same short rail in front of the cue ball one diamond closer toward the pocket, but make sure that *the blocker* is frozen to the rail. Place the object ball that you're going to pocket at the end of the same short rail at the corner pocket, let's say about two inches out from the pocket. Now you're going to elevate the butt of the cue stick at a forty-five-degree angle up off the table for this shot. You need the cue ball to turn or spin to the left around the blocker, so you will be striking (stroking) the cue ball on the left side but just a little in toward the front, about one eight of an inch. Hitting the cue ball at just that small fraction in front of it will cause it to run forward. With the cue stick still elevated, you need to have a smooth stroke when you strike the cue ball. Strike the cue ball halfway down from the top of the ball to the table. Use one half of a tip just left of center on the cue ball and the same amount toward the front of the cue ball. Strike it with a moderate, smooth stroke. The softer and the smoother you stroke this shot, the more action you're going to get out of the cue ball. Do not change your grip on the cue stick. The grip should be as if you were going to shoot a normal shot, with the only difference being that the cue stick is held at a different angle. The stroke is very important; you have to stroke this shot nice and smooth with a short follow-through, almost hitting the table with the cue stick tip. *Do not pull the cue stick back off the shot.* You need that follow-through. Now what will happen with the cue ball when struck with the cue stick? The cue ball will be pushed out to the right side because you're hitting the cue ball on the left side; therefore, the cue ball has to go right. Remember, shoot soft and smooth with a good follow through. If you find out that the cue ball is turning over into the object ball or hitting the object ball before the cue ball clears the object ball, aim just a little more to the right of the blocker to try to clear it. If the cue ball hits the blocker once again, you may have to stroke the cue ball with a little more speed, still maintaining a smooth stroke. If the cue ball doesn't turn over toward the object ball, make sure your stroke is not out of control but smooth. If you hit the cue ball without a good stroke, the cue ball will not react to the English you're trying to put on the cue ball. Check your stroke and your follow through. If you are struggling with your stroke just to pocket balls and getting shape, don't attempt to master this shot. You have to have a controlled stroke.

Long Massé

What is a massé shot? And what can you accomplish by using the massé? When can or should you use it? These are all very good questions. First, what is a massé? A massé is a shot in which you elevate the butt of the cue stick to cause the cue ball to curve around another object ball or a ball that is blocking you from shooting directly at the intended object ball that you're trying to pocket. What can you accomplish by having this particular shot in your arsenal? You can make shots when you can't use the jump cue because there are too many balls in front of the cue ball or you don't have a direct line to the object ball you're trying to pocket or maybe you don't own a jump cue. Say you're only a quarter of an inch to one side or behind a ball that's blocking you from pocketing the intended object ball. This is only one of several times you can use the massé shot. When performed properly, the massé shot will let you successfully curve the cue ball around the ball that's blocking the cue ball from hitting the intended object ball and pocket said ball.

To use this particular massé shot or to make the cue ball curve around the blocker (the ball in front of the cue ball), you should elevate the back or butt of the cue stick about three degrees up from a normal level or shooting position. The distance we're using between the blocker and the cue ball will prevent you from having to elevate the back of cue stick too much. In this particular shot we're starting at the lowest elevation for the back of the cue stick as needed. The reason that you raise the back of the cue roughly three degrees is that this shot is made for distance with the cue ball. If you raised the butt of the cue too much or a lot higher—say, at a forty-degree angle—the cue ball would turn in to the left or right so fast that the cue ball wouldn't get the distance you need to reach the object ball if the object ball is down the table more than five feet. So the lower the butt of the cue stick is, the more distance you'll get out of the shot. On this shot we're going to have to travel some distance to the object ball, so you need to have the cue stick lower to the table.

Use the center ball on the cue ball and then move the tip of the cue stick toward the bottom of the cue ball one full tip. Now move the tip of the cue stick one half tip over to the right, still at the bottom center of the cue ball. You will need a little distance between the blocker and the cue ball. Let's set up the shot. The cue ball will be to the left of the blocker but hidden behind it so that the cue ball has to be curved around the blocker to hit the object ball. Your cue ball is being blocked only by a quarter of an inch, and you can't see or pocket the intended object ball if you shoot the cue ball straight or directly at the object ball because you will hit the blocker. So without hitting the blocker that's in front of the cue ball, you must then curve the cue ball, or massé the cue ball. On this shot I'm describing, you need approximately two feet between the cue ball and the blocker. Place the cue ball down at one end of the table one diamond in from the short rail and then one diamond in from the rail on the right. Now place the blocker two diamonds in from the short rail and two diamonds in from the right rail toward the center of the table. Now place the object ball at the corner pocket down the table on the left side just out of the pocket about one or two inches. The distance between the cue ball and the blocker gives the cue ball time to work. When you strike the cue ball on the right side, the cue ball will be pushed out to the left and go around the blocker. The force that you put on the cue ball by hitting it to the right of center will cause it to spin to the right, which in turn will make the cue ball work back to the right and down the table to the object ball. Now, when you aim at the object ball that you want to pocket, aim just to the left side of the blocker as if you're going to nick the blocker when you hit the cue ball. The cue ball will first shoot out to the left just enough to clear the blocker and then start working back to the right, making contact with the object ball, and hopefully you'll pocket the ball. This shot requires a smooth and soft stroke with a good follow-through.

Now, let's say the blocker is three feet from the cue ball and hiding the cue ball by one half of an inch. The object ball is four feet from the blocker down the table at the corner pocket. This is one of those times that, because of the distance between the cue ball and the blocker and the portion of the cue ball that is being blocked, you want to elevate the cue stick butt at a fifteen-degree angle, or almost a third of the way up from the normal stroke. Because of the slightly higher elevation on the cue stick, the cue ball needs to have that little extra push to make it stay to the left a little longer so it will clear the blocker before it starts working back to the right. From a normal stroke to a straight up-and-down stroke, this would be just under one third of that distance off the table and the longest distance that you would have to curve the cue ball around a blocker. The massé shot can go straight up and down to flat, as in a normal stroke level, and everything in between. For longer shots the butt of the cue stick is lower, and for shorter shorts the cue stick is higher. Most long massé shots are made with the cue stick lower to the table as in a normal stroke if the blocker is more than a foot or so away. Try different elevations and see the difference in each shot.

Now let's get to the longer massé shot. On this shot you have a little more distance to cover. It depends on which side of the cue ball you need to strike with your English. If you need to go around the blocker to the left side, you need to hit or strike the cue ball with bottom right. Let's set the shot up. Place the cue ball one diamond in from the bottom rail and one diamond in from the rail on the right. The object ball or the blocker will be just up from the short rail where the cue ball is set but on the right rail in between the first and second diamond. Now push the cue ball in toward the middle of the table by one diamond. The blocker should be in front of the cue ball, blocking the cue ball from hitting the object by one quarter of an inch. You need to elevate the butt of the cue stick by at least halfway between the top and the bottom of the stroke. The angle of the cue stick is necessary so the cue ball will curve around the blocker. If you don't have the cue stick at this angle, the cue ball will not clear the blocker and will not have enough force to clear the blocker or make the curve. Strike the cue ball with a smooth stroke. Your cue stick needs to be at the bottom of the cue ball one full tip below the center of the cue ball. Now you're still at the bottom of the cue ball; move to the right one half of a tip. You don't need to aim the cue ball completely away from the blocker because you want to rely on the movement of the cue ball. Aim the cue ball *just enough* to clear the blocker. The movement of the cue ball will do the rest, going around the blocker when you hit the cue ball. So just aim slightly to the left; if you're confident, leave maybe an eighth of an inch of the object ball still blocking the cue ball. When you strike the cue ball with the downward motion with right English on the cue ball, the cue ball is going to be pushed or forced to the left. The English then will grab and begin to pull, or work, back to the right after the cue ball clears the object ball. Now use a moderate but smooth stroke, nothing too hard. See if you get the cue ball to clear the blocker—that's the first thing. The second thing is to see if the cue ball reacts to the right English that you're using and starts to curve or turn back to the right. If you hit the blocker, that could mean a number of things, such as that you didn't aim far enough out away from the blocker, you didn't shoot the cue ball quite hard enough, or you didn't smooth out your stroke. Also, you might not have raised the butt of the cue stick enough. Don't try to change all of these at once. Change one thing at a time and see how each change will improve the shot.

CHAPTER 14

CLOTH ON THE TABLE

Have you ever wondered why the cue ball won't travel as fast or as far as you would like it to? You might say that the table is just too slow and wonder why good players play just fine on the same table you play on. First of all, did you check the cloth of the table you're going to play on when you went into the building? How do you check the cloth? Just place your hand on the table and run it along the felt to assess the playing surface. Is the surface of the table smooth? If so, the table will play pretty fast. But let's check one other thing. What is the weight of the cue ball? If it is heavy, then the table will run a little bit faster still.

When you feel that the surface of the table is rough—when you can feel the nap—that roughness will prevent the cue ball from running in a straight line. If you try to hit the cue ball really slow, it will run even slower that you intended because of the friction from the nap. So you're right—the table is going to play pretty slow.

If the cue ball is heavy, this means two things. The cue ball is going to be hard to control, so you will have to use a little more English because the cue ball will want to stay in motion after making contact with the object ball if hit with high English. And with any slow English,shots the surface of the table will grab the ball and move it a lot faster in the direction you want the English to go.

There are two other things to consider. If the weather outside is cold and wet, what do you think about playing on a table close to the entrance of the pool room? The tables closer to the door will be affected by the weather. They will be slower in wet weather because of the moisture in the air coming from outside. In hot weather, those tables will play faster because they will be dried out and more firm.

These are some of the things to consider when you enter the pool room. If you want a faster table, then look for a smoother cloth. If you want a slower table, find one with cloth that is a little rougher. Also consider the weather and the weight of the cue ball. And remember—practice, practice, practice.

CHAPTER 15

HOW TO JUDGE YOUR SPEED OFF THE OBJECT BALL

In judging the speed you need to get from the cue ball to the object ball and then to pocket that ball, you have to consider the cloth itself, whether it is smooth or rough. You will have to use either more English to run the cue ball to get it to the second object ball, or you will have to shoot just a little harder to move the cue ball to where you need it to go. The smoother surface will cause very little friction to slow the cue ball from running rail to rail. You need to be careful about how much English you use when the surface of the table is smooth. Friction occurs when two surfaces (the outside of an object or body, meaning the cue ball and the table) rub against each other. Heat will result from the rubbing. So when you get to your local pool room, feel some of the table surfaces. The faster tables will be nice and smooth, while the slower tables will not be so smooth. On a fast table, you want to use less English and cut back your speed on your stroke and your follow through. You will notice differences in all of your shots. You won't need as much follow through as you would on a slower table. The cue ball will react with every follow through. If the follow through is just a little too much, you will see a huge reaction, so cut down your follow through on a faster table. It's just the opposite on a table that is slower; you're going to have to use a little more follow through and a little more English to get the job done. Don't think that you have to pick up your speed with the cue stick. Just use a little more English and follow through. Practice, practice, practice, and never give up on yourself.

ABOUT THE AUTHOR

George Moyle is seventy years old and still playing tournaments locally. I have also played in a nine-ball tournament in Lincoln City, Oregon, where there were two hundred players in my bracket. I was one match from the finals when I was beaten. I still made some money and had a good time. I have yet to be back to Lincoln City because of health problems, but those problems are all behind me now. Since then, I have played local tournaments. I have won every tournament I have entered within a fifty-mile radius of my home. I grew up in a small town where there wasn't really much to do, so my mom got me into baseball at a young age. That was my game at the time. Little did I know that I also had the desire to play pool. Little League was my passion then, and I was good. Then came basketball, football, and other sports, but hardball was the sport at which I excelled. Then one day after church, everybody got together at a friend's house for a potluck lunch. Under the homeowner's three-car carport was a pool table. I was fascinated. At that time, I was twelve years old, and I asked if I could play. One of the guys said sure and that I could be on his team. This was my first encounter with a sport that I knew nothing about, and it was so much fun. Just hitting those balls around was thrilling. Every time we had potluck at the same house, guess what I wanted to do? Play pool. It got to the point that pool was addictive. I wanted to play more and more. So I asked the homeowner, whose name was Mary, if I could come and play once in a while. She said, "As long as you put things back where they go." She had no problem with my playing pool, even when they weren't home. So when I wasn't playing baseball, I was playing pool.

When I got into my teens, I started going to the local pool hall where I would meet a few friends, and I started learning more about the game. But I had a lot of questions. What would happen if I hit the cue ball like this? That was something I had never tried before. The cue ball didn't even come close to the object ball that I was trying to pocket. I missed the pocket by a mile. This started me thinking: *What just happened?* So I tried the same thing again, but there was different action on the cue ball this time. Talk about trying to use English. I was lost from the get-go. But later in my teens, I starting learning more and more about English and some of what English can do. I asked for help from some of the better players, but they either didn't know how or didn't want to teach anyone. After spending thousands of hours on the pool table, I taught myself about English and why it is so important to the game. Without English, you can get yourself in trouble. English will keep you out of trouble, but English will also get you into trouble. English will get you back in line also. It's a wonderful game. Be patient with yourself, but have some fun. I hope this book has answered some of the questions that you have. I hope to see you out there. Practice, practice practice! Never give up on yourself.

Printed in the United States
By Bookmasters